Branding to Differ

The Brand Building Handbook for Business Leaders

JEAN-LUC AMBROSI

LIBERUM PRESS

First published 2014 by Liberum Press, Melbourne, Australia.
www.liberumpress.com

National Library of Australia Cataloguing-in-Publication entry:

Author:	Ambrosi, Jean-Luc, author.
Title:	Branding to differ / Jean-Luc Ambrosi.
ISBN:	9780992293604 (hbk.)
Notes:	Includes index.
Subjects:	Branding (Marketing)
	Marketing.
	658.827

Typeset in Agora Sans and Diplomat Sans

To the members of my family,
those who are no longer here and
the ones who fill my life today.

66

Products are created in the factory,
but brands are created in the mind."

Walter Landor

Contents

"

A fun brand with a grumpy service operative
is not a fun brand – it's a grumpy brand."

CHAPTER 1

Living the dream

Branding is by far the most talked about subject in marketing. It is also a subject about which everyone shares an opinion: marketers and non-marketers, consumers, business leaders, passers-by. We love some brands and love to hate others. We trust some and distrust others. We emulate the behaviours they affirm. We relate to them, we have opinions and ... we have feelings about them.

What is generating such enthusiasm when, in essence, branding is mostly conceptual? I must admit that for many years the brand concept eluded my comprehension. Of course, I could articulate brand generalities like any marketing graduate, even sound knowledgeable. But the essence, the fundamental understanding of what is a brand, somehow eluded me. To really comprehend what a brand is and where its true power resides I had to approach the concept in two ways. The first was to look at the effect of brands in terms of their relationship to consumer perceptions, purchase behaviours and consumer responses; how these are linked to brands. It was obvious that the perception of the benefits associated with a brand affects consumer behaviour in many ways, sometimes far beyond the direct product benefits. Brands are affecting the way people interact, purchase, remain loyal, talk about and promote products. Brands are also able to drive pricing differentials.

A second insight came from my psychology background. I began to realise that while brands have a measurable effect on consumer behaviour, they merely represent a symptom of something more important. This led me to develop a specific conceptual framework, which I call the Brand Projection Framework. Brands are really a perception, or what psychologists call a 'projection' – a projection of a personal expectation, feeling or dream about an object. If things go well for the brand, it will become an object of desire. Psychology defines this as the unconscious attribution of a personal thought, feeling, or impulse to somebody else, or something else. In reality, the brand does not exist. It is only a representation, with both a rational and an emotional component that has strong links to personal desires, needs, wants, fears and aspirations. Yet it can be potent when it meets our aspirations, or satisfies our wants and dreams. The rational component is the promise of a concrete output: 'a reliable car' for example. The emotional component is the link to our aspirations: 'a car which will make me look successful'. To manage their brands, therefore, organisations need to understand not only the intrinsic value of the products they carry and how they meet concrete expectations. They also need to know what the products represent in the customers' minds, what expectations or dreams they fulfil – and must keep fulfilling.

Living the dream

Today, the word "brand" has evolved to encompass uniqueness; it defines the individuality of a product, a company or a service. It drives an array of perceptions and feelings. It can, in turn, speak about immediate and achievable benefits (such as consuming fast moving consumer goods products for example) or unachievable dreams such as winning the lottery.

While the foundation of a brand remains the same, the added value it can bring to organisations has taken on proportions never seen before. According to the World Intellectual Property Organisation, a company's intangible assets, including its brand, can represent up to 80 percent of its corporate value[1]. This signifies that brands themselves can become drivers of financial value for corporations expanding their balance sheets and moving total value beyond simple book value.

1   2011 World Intellectual Property report. The changing face of innovation. WIPO Economics & Statistics Series. World Intellectual Property Organisation.

66

Mixing of art and science is often
the way great brands are built."

CHAPTER 2

Ten seconds of history

Brands were initially developed for a very specific purpose. Originally they were created to mark cattle with a hot iron to determine to whom the cattle belonged. The cattle were 'branded' with a name or initials, 'the logo'. The purpose was to differentiate one cow from another for ownership and management purposes. Such differentiation was necessary because most cattle looked like, well, cattle.

While the earliest forms of branding can be traced to ancient societies' use of symbols or characters to distinguish ownership of goods, branding did not really take on its full significance until the 19th century. The rise of corporate entities, which made products available to growing groups of middle class individuals, meant that trademarking and branding was brought to the masses. With industrialisation, the emergence of widely recognised brands in packaged goods and other manufactured products started to appear. From then on, the role of branding would develop beyond signifying ownership, it became an indicator of meanings and added benefits.

Branding has evolved since those early days but the initial idea has prevailed. It is a way to differentiate a product, or a group of products, from other products with similar characteristics or from a similar category. A brand is one of the tools used to be a key differentiator. A brand promises to meet expectations and provide benefits that are different from the other products or brands in one way or another.

It is thus important to tread with caution when managing a brand, its components and its image. Brands must be managed strategically. 'Airy fairy' marketing habits, uninformed managers, personal opinions and the application of 'creative juices' out of context are no longer acceptable. Branding is part of the business strategy – not the strategy department but the true business strategy embraced by the organisation. Above all, it reflects the business vision. At that point, and that point only, does the creativity of managing the brand come in. So it is up to marketing managers or business managers to set the vision, the foundation of the brand. Later will come the time for ideas, creativity and logos.

"

A great brand is a brand that allows your sales people to open prospects' doors, to add the convincing touch to a pitch, to convince prospects that the pricing premium is justified.

That is, to reinforce the entire sales process. It is the ultimate enabler of sales which will always raise the challenge of mixing short term sales objectives with longer term brand sustainability."

CHAPTER 3

What is Branding?

It is important not to confuse the mechanisms used to develop a brand and the concept of branding itself. To be clear: branding is not advertising. Advertising is a mechanism to support a branding effort. It may or may not be used to develop brand awareness. It is simply a medium used for promoting the brand, its products or its services. In the same fashion a logo, or 'look & feel' are just identifiers. They are a quick image that helps customers recognise everything the brand stands for. Again, it is not branding per se but a support mechanism whose purpose, in this instance, is to identify the brand.

One can define branding in many way but we need to be clear about what the meaning of branding is. I would like to propose this definition:

Branding is a succinct articulation of a meaningful promise to customers that is clear and different to what your competitors provide.

What this implies is that by being the articulation or expression of a promise, a brand is just a psychological concept. It is the driver of a perception, whether based in fact or fiction.

Conceptually the brand is built on two pillars. The first concerns the values that the brand conveys and the second is the promise to the end user.

These two essential components are necessary to build the brand image because they carry both the rational and emotional components needed for the brand to be accepted by the end user. The values aspect relates to what or who is the brand. What does it stand for, how is it characterised, and what feelings or emotions does it generate? The promise relates to what the brand aims to deliver to its customers. Not only from a product delivery point of view but also in terms of its overall suggestiveness. This is something that is far more encompassing. What will this brand deliver to me, the customer? What expectations will it fulfil, how will it make me feel? If I purchase a very expensive shirt from a renowned brand, for example, what I will get is not just a shirt, but potentially the promise to look great, to be recognised for my

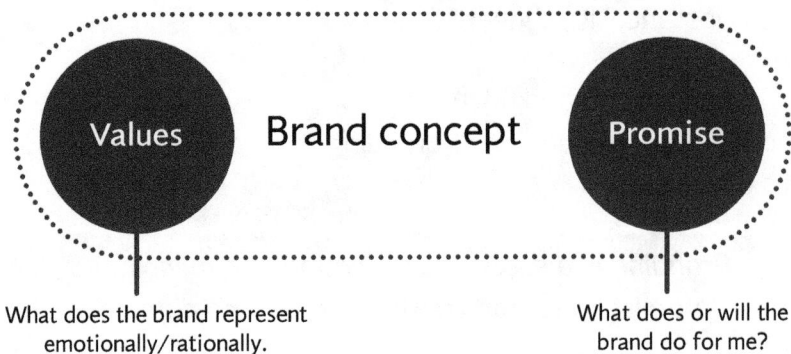

Values   **Brand concept**   Promise

What does the brand represent
emotionally/rationally.

What does or will the
brand do for me?

good taste, or to be seen as a successful individual, able to get the best that life has to offer. This is the promise, a point at which the rational mind may get taken over by emotion. The brand promise is at a minimum about fulfilling our needs and desires. It can also be about fulfilling our intimate wishes and dreams. The more the brand is about dreams, the more 'ethereal' the brand construction and promise of delivery will be. The high end world of fashion is very much about delivering dreams. It is reflected in all aspects of the brand approach: from the star status of fashion designers, to the fabulous store experience, to the high end media exposure, to the glossiness of the advertising, to the vocabulary used to describe the brand or its products. As we see, this goes far beyond (and sometimes doesn't even include) a logo or advertising. The entire brand experience is kept consistent. Extreme care is being taken to ensure that all outputs are developed to support the brand image and the dream it evokes.

Brand personality

While on the subject of psychological concepts, many marketers and psychologists also like to use the term brand personality to define brands. I must mention it here as it is widely discussed but seldom mastered. This concept is roughly based on 'The Big-Five Model' of human personality defined by a number of psychologists (with Lewis R. Goldberg as one of the most cited[2]). Simply put a brand personality is just a set of characteristics defining the brand that have human like traits. The theory behind this is that people relate better to personalities similar to them. This concept is useful to help define brand direction and can be a great tool to drive people from different areas and backgrounds throughout an organisation as it is very easy to understand. But it also difficult to master as the psychology research has been oversimplified or even 'bastardised' when applied to brand, with different research studies showing that these oversimplified models rarely work. As psychologists defined the Big Five: Extroversion, Agreeableness, Conscientiousness, Emotional Stability, and Openness; Brand 'experts' created: Excitement, Sincerity, Ruggedness, Competence and Sophistication. Perhaps something to do with the fact that branding people are often extroverts and think they are exciting..? Of course great brands go beyond the personality concept and when necessary create their own personality models if they find it useful as a tool. What is important to remember is that the use of the brand personality concept is only useful if it facilitates the introduction of the Values and the Promise throughout the organisation as a tool.

2 (Goldberg, L. R. (1990). An alternative "Description of personality": The Big-Five
   factor structure. Journal of Personality and Social Psychology, 59, 1216-1229)

66

If you stand for 'something', your decisions
are guided by this 'something'. What you
do, what you offer, how you behave must
be congruent with this 'something."

CHAPTER 4

Characteristics of organisations with successful branding

Best practice? We often hear the term best practice used when referring to brand management. But is there really such a thing, and if there is, how do we define it?

More often than not the term best practice will refer to one aspect of brand management such as the vision, strategy, strategic process, the implementation framework or particular aspects of the implementation and output generation. Do not get distracted by this use of best practice to describe a process. Best practice, from a positioning, vision and strategy point of view, requires the creation of a clear point of difference. To achieve a clear point of difference for the organisation it is not a bad idea to do things differently from the start.

Today's successful brands are often referred to as examples of best practice to follow. Brands like Apple, Coca Cola, and Google are commonly cited as worthy of emulation. A few decades ago it was Kodak, IBM, Porsche and a few others, some of which have disappeared, as has the iconic Pan Am. Strength today may not always be a recipe for tomorrow's success. Brands are part of a complex eco system in which product relevance, economic and social factors and timing all play a role in their success or failure. Brand management, at least in its traditional form, is only one part of the equation.

Today, brand management must sit with the overall business strategy and vision that steer the entire organisation. This is why I am a strong advocate for having marketing executives (the traditional brand guardians) sitting at the executive table to ensure the decisions that affect the brand are made within a holistic framework that encompasses both short and long term perspectives. This, in turn, raises questions about the role of marketing in the brand management process. No matter how we want to define best practice, the role of marketing must encompass strategic visioning for the whole organisation. It must be able to be, at times, at the helm. It must always be a continuous and active participant. The worst possible scenario is to have the marketing department concentrating only on specific outputs (the usual suspects being logo, 'look and feel' and advertising) as opposed to providing an all encompassing direction for all parts of the organisation.

A little caution is required with how the term 'best practice' is used due to the evolutionary nature of brand management and the number of variables to consider when dealing with the entire brand management process. I will therefore refer to best practice for specific components or methodologies, such as the communication process. Most relevant are the attributes shared by successful brands; whether these are called 'best practice' or 'key characteristics'. Let's have a look at the model.

The 9 characteristics of organisations with successful branding

1. Moving beyond the marketing responsibility

The modus operandi of branding is to provide a way to integrate the business in a way that is inclusive of corporate culture, communications, products and services. Each of these components in isolation does not constitute branding. But the sum of these make up a brand—a culture, a direction, a way of doing things. Marketing departments can lead in the effort to build, maintain and reinforce these dimensions of a brand. Yet on its own, the marketing department will only have a limited impact in most cases. The brand experience for consumers needs to be delivered consistently, in its entirety or at least consistently, during critical moments, the 'moments of truth'. It is the entire experience, of critical moments of interaction with the brand, that really matter in the consumer's eyes. It is necessary for the organisation to cater for these experiences throughout their different touch points. All areas in which the company interacts with consumers, or has an impact on customers, must be considered part of the brand strategy.

2. Making marketing a driver

Marketing must be a driver of strategy, tactics and information. The key word is 'driver'. The worst scenario is one where marketing is a reactive function, responding to business needs and demands but not providing the organisation with a strategic and tactical view. The late David Packard, co-founder of Hewlett-Packard once made the comment that *"marketing is too important to be left to the marketing department"*. This is also true for branding. Unless marketing is able to provide strategic and tactical leadership, key information and the ability to think beyond the walls of the marketing department to look at the organisation as a whole, the brand will not be effective. So why should marketing be a driver? A key function of marketing is to manage and promote the brand. When done properly marketing monitors the value of the brand and is able to alert the business or steer it away from actions that would have a detrimental effect. In most scenarios the marketing department becomes somewhat obsessive with the brand. It monitors its progression, it steers the activities that support it, it communicates with the other business areas and it acts at the 'door bitch' restraining anyone who breaks the branding rules. These activities contribute to keeping the brand top of mind, ensuring consistency. To use a metaphor from psychology, it enables the brand to avoid schizophrenic behaviours: messages that contradict each other or that lack a high level of coherence.

3. Having the brand championed by senior management externally and internally

This is absolutely key. If the brand is not championed at the highest levels, it will make the task of developing the full potential of the brand almost impossible. Unless the brand is considered to be of paramount importance by the senior executives, decisions will be made without thorough consideration of the impact on the brand. Over time this will systematically steer the brand away from its core promise resulting in a lack of brand focus, a loss of the essence of the brand, and that which makes the organisation and its products 'different'. No marketing campaign, advertising, slogan, change of name or logo, or any other tactic, can replace the need for top management championship. The 'promises' made via the different marketing mediums and sales touch points, will start sounding hollow because a dichotomy between the reality and the promises will emerge and widen. Therefore senior leaders must embrace the brand and what it stands for to ensure that the organisation as a whole is engaged and is working towards the same goal. *It is the role of senior leaders to share the mission of the brand.* It is paramount for senior leaders to carry the message inside the organisation, day in day out. From a pure brand perspective this is their key role: to drive belief in the brand and above all bolster staff engagement. It is also very desirable for leaders to carry the brand message outside the organisation. Witness the impact created by leaders like Steve Jobs and Richard Branson. Equally, leaders need to understand their own constraints and decide which audience they will direct their messages to. Their first audience must always consist of their own stakeholders to ensure that their vision is adopted, whether it is the board of directors, the management team, shareholders and staff or other stakeholders. How the brand message is carried outside the organisation is another step. There is a difference between managing an organisation and its brand and being the flag bearer for the brand. The former is a business leadership skill, the latter is a communication skill. While we can encourage leaders to develop their external communication abilities, if this is not their main playing field they should only participate in specific communication efforts when they are able to add real value as opposed to an all-encompassing communication effort which will require enormous commitment in time and effort.

4. Making the brand a driver for business decisions

The brand should not be subordinate to specific business decisions. If you stand for 'something', your decisions are guided by this 'something'. What you do, what you offer, how you behave must be congruent with this 'something'. Of course, in the real world many forces are at play that may steer the leadership of organisations into different strategies and behaviours. This is not an issue as long as the 'something' is always included in the balance. Depending on what the 'something' is, it will have more or less impact on the decision process. For example if you stand first for customer satisfaction—the way you staff call centres, build your telephony routing process or train the staff—will be based on maximising the quality of the customer experience. Going for the absolutely cheapest solution may contradict your value proposition, your special 'something'. Alternately, if your value proposition is first to provide low costs, then choosing the cheapest solutions could well be aligned with your overall value proposition. Many of the telecommunication companies who strongly compete on price deliberately have a low servicing approach. While it may not always please their customer base it is congruent with the 'promise'. What the organisation stands for is critical in the decision making process, so when leaders decide on a clear value proposition, all the elements that affect the experience of the customers must be taken into account. Great brands do not always have great service or a great footprint, or great advertising, or a great product. As the management gurus teach us: Pick your battle.

IBM provides a great example of disassociation of the brand from its physical products. The sale of its PC division to China-based Lenovo could have easily been seen as a fragmentation of the brand. On the contrary it freed capital, allowing IBM to move from selling what had become commoditised products at low-margins, to selling high-value solutions and services. This high value component had always been a trait of IBM and in some ways IBM was going back to its origins. By undertaking this shift, IBM did not get caught up in the products they were selling. They realised that the products were not the brand but only a reflection of what the brand could offer. Instead, IBM remained true to its brand spirit of a high quality and innovative offering. Of course when the organisation was created IBM leaders probably never thought they could offer anything else than computers as the core offering, otherwise they may not have called themselves International Business Machines. But IBM was able to shift away from one of its core product offerings while remaining true to its brand spirit. That is not to say that the product is insignificant. In fact, most brands have been built solely through the selling and promoting of a product or a range of products and services.

Some brands actually never speak of the brand, only of its products. But when the product and the brand are getting too far apart, when a disconnect arises, the brand owner has a choice. The brand can be repositioned to suit the product or product lines. Or the product can be changed to suit the brand. The latter is less frequent, which is why the IBM example is of particular interest.

5. Ensuring the brand is embraced within the organisation by all employees

A fun brand with a grumpy service operative is not a fun brand – it's a grumpy brand. The only way to ensure that all customer touch points reflect the essence of the brand is to engage all staff and make them "live the brand". Today, consumers are pretty quick to see the "spin". Once burned, they will seldom come back. Your employees will embrace the brand if the promise can be delivered. Building a brand promise that cannot be delivered will only reduce staff engagement and put the credibility of the brand offering at risk.

How many organisations promise a world of great service and opportunities to their clients and prospects only to deliver sub-standard service due to understaffing and poor resourcing? What this does in the long run is to create a dichotomy between the promise and the reality. It ends up with the message, and ultimately the brand, being discredited. Organisations should make sure that their promises match what is delivered so that staff can 'live the brand' and feel part of the brand promise. Logic and research shows that engaged staff are more likely to deliver a better experience to customers than those who are not engaged.

6. Making sure the brand is reflected throughout all customer outputs

The proof is in the pudding. The brand DNA must be shared and reflected through most, if not all, interactions with consumers and prospective customers. A common issue, which most of us would have experienced, is a discrepancy between the marketing or sales promise and the level of delivery. If your brand is "fun", then your staff must embody the "fun". So must your communication, your packaging, and your servicing. A modern brand must employ modern engagement methods such as online interaction or paying attention to details such as well-designed invoices or phone call response mechanisms. All moments of interaction have an effect on the customer experience and the customer's assessment of the brand. Great brands do not confine the brand experience to marketing and sales messaging. They reflect the brand experience through diverse interactions, even the most benign ones.

7. Segmentation Awareness

Successful brands place particular emphasis on customer segmentation. This is true from both a customer behaviour analysis perspective and from an attitudinal study perspective. With the advance in database management in the 1980s and 1990s, we saw the building of a raft of tools that made it possible for marketers to analyse, comprehend and predict aspects of customer behaviours. This 'power of knowledge' provides an edge to organisations, providing support to the decision making process. The knowledge takes two basic forms: an understanding of consumer behaviour and a relative ability to predict behaviour.

Understanding customer behaviour is however a difficult task. The use of data can demonstrate how consumers react to different variables placed in front of them like price reductions, special offers, change in packaging, use of marketing mediums or communication techniques. For example how will they react to specific offers, via which channels of communication? Which form of communication and creative execution in the short term will they respond to? Analysing data this way is an essential tool for tactical decision making, allowing AB testing, challenger testing etc (e.g. does offer A work better than offer B?). It allows us to understand what variables or group of variables have an impact on the decision making process and purchase behaviours. The key in these instances is good reliable data, which is essential. It is also where most failures occur. If the data is not reliable, look elsewhere. Most successful brands understand this and spend a vast amount of effort cleansing their data and ensuring the reliability of whatever data source they wish to analyse. Good data does not always require expensive data warehousing or CRM systems. Good data means the source is known to be reliable. It has been properly entered and properly stored, discrepancies have been cleansed or removed, the data repository is safe and sturdy and the tools used to capture the data are capturing the precise variables required.

The understanding of customers is not just linked to data of course, but the use of data has propelled marketing departments to the forefront of business decision making, enabling them to have a voice at the most senior levels. It has enabled them to display an understanding of customers and to show the ability to build return on investment mechanisms. Good usage of data requires discipline and an understanding of what statistical analysis means and does not mean. It is a tool that must be used in context; extrapolations can be dangerous and often misguided. Data that tracks past behaviour is used to develop understanding of customer behaviour and to devise future strategies. It can also be used to track present behaviour, for immediate action. The availability of real time behavioural data, including purchase behaviour, especially online, allows marketers to manage and refine campaigns and company offers. This data can be extremely useful to test and improve on customers' activities, whether it be acquisition, retention or cross selling. What it doesn't do, however, is provide an understanding of brand impact, the longer term effect of current activities. Therefore the use of data for immediate activities must be assessed differently from overall brand data. For example increasing sales via special offers can have a positive or negative impact on the brand. The use of the special offer may drive immediate sales and better brand awareness in the short term, but devalue the positioning of the brand in the longer term.

Understanding brand impact often requires a more longitudinal approach, whereby behaviours and attitudes are monitored over a period of time. The brand manager must always know how to differentiate short term impacts from trends. Trends will indicate whether the brand is moving in the right direction. It will provide the first clues about whether action is required to continue, alter or change the existing strategy. The trend analysis must be meticulous as the choice of different time horizons might lead to very different conclusions. A long upward trend (say 3-5 years) should be questioned if the short term trend (3-6 months) is negative. Both need to be weighed against each other within the market context. How does the organisational trend compare to the market trend, or to past activities at similar periods? While this type of analysis is used every day in business strategy, great brands will assess the brand impact of the different trends affecting the organisation and not just their financial impact. This allows the organisation to focus on the value or perceived value that the brand provides, now and in the future.

After the analysis of brand attributes over time, the real 'joker' in the pack of successful brand building lies in the ability to define tangible customer and prospect segments. Being 'segment aware' means that the brand can be made to cater for specific types of customers and customer needs. Having the ability to define segments and cater for these segments is a crucial evolution in the life of a brand. Most marketers and business leaders know that the one-for-all approach has its limitations. Understanding to whom your brand appeals, and to whom it does not appeal, provides one of the most powerful tools to driving successful brands.

There are a wide number of ways in which to define segments. A multi-level approach to segmentation is crucial:

1. Visualising

The first stage is for defining a high level image enabling brand managers to visualise the core target audiences' attributes. What consumer category, what type of people do we want to attract, what drives the purchase motivation, who are they and what do they look like, what differentiates them? This can be done in a number of ways but basically two approaches dominate: behavioural segmentation and attitudinal segmentation.

> *Behavioural segmentation* is based on data that has been gathered either internally through activity tracking of purchase behaviour, or externally through analysis of customer behaviour. What this analysis provides is a group of variables that can be used to build one or many profiles of the type of customers using the brand. The more information available (directly or appended) the more precise the profiles will be. This form of analysis provides clues as to 'who' are the brand customers. It may also provide clues as to 'what' activities they react to. The main advantage of this form of analysis is that it provides factual data. It can also enable the building of models that will create a brand mechanism to reach people with the desired attributes.

Attitudinal segmentation aims to determine 'why' customers use the brand. The advantage of this approach is that it provides insights into the decision making process of customers and prospects. It aims at defining motivational attributes. The disadvantage of this approach is that it can sometimes be based on superficial evidence and provide a less than accurate picture unless it is properly done. I have seen countless pieces of evidence of attitudinal data based on a set of pre-conceptions and clichés. To avoid this, one must use a reliable research firm to manage qualitative and quantitative research appropriately. The most obvious disadvantage resides in the fact that it is often difficult, and sometimes impossible, to reach people with these attributes accurately.

II. Targeting

The second stage is concentrated on pure targeting. It is about defining purpose built segments based on a set of variables that can be used to reach individuals with more than an average propensity to accept your offer. This will not provide an 'image' of your segments but it is a targeting methodology which is very distinctive from the previous segmentation. In my experience purpose built segments, that is segments built for a single targeting objective (e.g. acquisition, retention), are more efficient than all-encompassing segments. While the variables they use may not provide an 'image 'of the individuals, they provide information relevant to increase the effectiveness of the targeting effort. Ultimately, the significance and arrangement of these variables provides the model on which to define more likely targets, targets with a higher than average propensity to purchase. There is no need during this stage to visualise the audience. As long as these groups fit within the high level segments (which has already provided an image of the group of individuals composing the segments), this targeting exercise involves finding and reaching high potential prospects and customers. In particular, when customer or prospect data is available, it can be used to build algorithms to select relevant data sets for targeting. The data driven effort is based on identifying which variables are significant when defining propensity measures. The purpose is to reach high potential prospects or customers, as opposed to defining what high potential looks like. This is an important point to make as the two are often confused. Managers want to put a face on aggregate data. This exercise is futile as the aggregate will change as the model evolves. What really matters is the importance of the core variables in the targeting process. If these variables are meaningful (for example men living in postcode 3006) all the better. But if not (for example people having reached a website destination more than 2.7 times and coming from concurrent websites) what matters is the ability to reach the audience and to deliver a message that will promote the brand in a customised fashion.

The impacts of segmentation

Segmentation is often misunderstood because it comprises a number of different processes designed to suit different purposes. We can summarize these as follows:

Understanding
1. Understanding your audience, their characteristics, what makes them different (or not). What particular attributes define them?

2. Understanding what attracts your audience and the different segments that make up your audience and what draws them to the different products offered by the brand.

3. Understanding the triggers that drive your audience to act. Purchase triggers, promoter triggers etc.

Targeting

This is the ability to define and find customers and prospective customers who are most likely to purchase your products or adopt your brand. It is often based on the concept of attracting people with similar profiles to your existing customers (so current offerings as future offerings may attract different people and may require a different approach).

Impacting

This is defining what is the best way to reach and communicate with the prospects and customer groups. What type of message, or offer, what tone or medium of communication etc. will most likely attract these segments?

Measuring

What is the effect of your activities (or lack of) on your customers and prospects? What are the short term, medium term and long term (trends) effects of your activities and strategy? What are the lessons learned? What needs to remain, what needs to be improved, what needs to change?

8. Moving from maximum intuition to maximum tracking

Great brands are often associated with great leaders. These leaders tend to share one trait in common: they drive a Vision. This Vision is not always grandiose or long term but it usually does derive from a deep understanding of the market in which they are involved, or from what is often described as "instinct". These leaders drive a movement, an impetus to create, in a manner that enables them to share and convince others with their Vision or objectives. While this is an essential element to creating a brand (and I won't spend much time on this, as others have studied this in far more detail) it is evident that successful brands cannot rely forever on one person's Vision. In the longer term, a complex system of understanding of the market and of the customers, must be at the core of these organisations' capacity to create sustainability. The understanding of customers, market participants and market dynamics is an essential element in the success of brands. Such understanding may reside in different parts of the organisation, often in the corporate strategy function. The brand strategy must reflect and base its approach on this understanding, otherwise it soon becomes irrelevant and out of touch with the organisation—and, more importantly, with customers.

The steps to create sustainable brands must therefore include a Vision that will drive and differentiate the offer and value proposition. But this will not be enough. To steer the brand for the longer term a tracking mechanism will be necessary to help provide insights and factual information about the brand, assess the impact of the organisation's actions and activities, and observe the evolution of the market. In other words, the *mixing of art and science is often the way great brands are built*.

9. Keeping brand development in a healthy relationship to sales*

One of the worst mistakes marketers and 'brand owners' can make is to treat the brand as a separate entity from the reality of the organisation especially when it comes to sales effectiveness. Independent of who drives sales for the organisation, whether it be senior management, the sales team, the marketing team or a third party, if your brand is not helping to sell more or better—that is in the way you want to sell, for example with a price premium—then your brand has, in effect, little value. Its contribution to the bottom line is not effective. Sure, marketers have the difficult task to take the brand beyond the very short term sales objectives that may sometimes devalue the brand in its long term ability to drive sales in the way the organisation wants to sell.

Marketers and brand owners must therefore ask themselves two key strategic questions when they build their brand strategy and their related tactical implementation.

1. Do the brand strategy and tactics support the organisation in the medium and long term, beyond this week, this month, this quarter or this year's objective?

---

* I have chosen the word sales as a core objective. The understanding of the prime objective in most organisations revolves around financial rewards. I use the word sales in the wider sense of the term to include customer acquisition, retention, cross sell and up-selling. This word can be used for organisations whose core objectives are not bottom line driven. For example lobbyists may look for "stakeholder impact", not for profit.

2. Will the brand strategy and its tactical implementation drive sales, retention or the ability to sell here and now?

If the answer to these question is 'Yes' then the next step is to understand how the strategies and related tactics can be integrated with the activities of the teams responsible for driving sales. These often will be the sales teams, customer service or marketing teams. Typically, they will focus on acquisition, up-selling and cross selling strategies and the driving of retention efforts. Often, they will have a short term focus. The role of the brand is to support the sales in the short and long term. Brand efforts must be looked at in the context of how they will support sales today, tomorrow and the day after. This means that brand messaging and brand activity must be adding value to the sales process today but equally it must not be compromised by short term considerations. Ultimately, it must drive traffic to the sales mechanisms: a web site, store, call centre or sales team. It must support the sales pitch, the after sales experience, the building of loyalty and the entire sales process. A level of integration is necessary, either in the form of a core message that is repeated via different channels or by the use of different messages adapted to each channel and which reinforce each other. For example a brand message focusing on trust could be an ideal precursor to a sales pitch. In this instance the brand message is setting the scene and allowing the sales message to focus on product benefits. A great brand is a brand that allows your sales people to open prospects' doors, to add the convincing touch to a pitch, to convince prospects that the pricing premium is justified. That is, to reinforce the entire sales process. It is the ultimate enabler of sales which will always raise the challenge of mixing short term sales objectives with longer term brand sustainability.

If the answer is 'No' to the two questions – that is, it is neither driving long term objectives nor short-term sales – you really need to ask yourself what is the purpose of the brand strategy?

"

Can you communicate your vision in less than thirty seconds? If the answer is 'Yes' you have more chance to have it understood, memorised and entrenched in the customers' minds."

CHAPTER 5

Starting point – or how do you build a brand

How do you develop a model to build a successful brand? Where do you start? What are the steps that an organisation should take or be cognisant of?

There are five core steps:

1. Vision and purpose

Defining what you have to offer. This includes developing: 'What we stand for', 'Who we want to be?', 'Where do we make a difference?' In other words, what is the brand's reason for being and how it is relevant to customers? The answer to these questions should remain short and focused and, above all, be able to be understood by all the people involved. Defining the vision and purpose must ring true to the people building the brand and these should not drastically change in the short term. A good example of a brand vision is the Amazon approach: "Our vision is to be earth's most customer centric company; to build a place where people can come to find and discover anything they might want to buy online." It is clear and to the point, defines a purpose, a point of differentiation and a channel of activities.

To be most effective vision statements should be brief and concise, focused, memorable, and self-explanatory. Avoid statements that are convoluted, unfocused, too long and difficult to understand. An easy test to perform is the thirty second spiel. Can you communicate your vision in less than thirty seconds? If the answer is 'Yes' you have more chance to have it understood, memorised and entrenched in the customers' minds.

2. Leadership and culture

To build a great brand you need to lead the values that underpin it from the top. These should be derived from the vision and purpose, until they are embedded within the organisation. The whole organisation needs to live and breathe these values. Senior managers as well as junior staff must champion them at all times. When people in the organisation think about the organisation's products, services or way of conducting business, they need to ensure that all these different aspects that drive and make up the business are synchronised with the culture. For example, if the purpose of an organisation is to develop products that enhance the well being of its customers, then all interactions with customers should be stress free. Products should be designed first with this objective in mind and the legitimate pursuit for profit should be weighted against the brand's purpose. I can hear voices in the background echoing scepticism about this particular point. "Deliver a well packaged product and they will come to you," they say. Perhaps they will, perhaps they will not. But if they do, will they come back if they have a bad experience or an experience not matching their expectations? Will they recommend your brand to their friends and families?

Great brands all have in common the fact that their customers will purchase again from them; repeat purchase is necessary for the longevity of the brand. They also tend to have high Net Promoter Scores (NPS) which means that their customers are recommending their products to third parties, increasing the footprint of the brand organically. Take the example of a very well-known brand like Apple. When you go to an Apple store, the fit- out of the store corresponds with the design of the products, as do the T-shirts the staff wear, and the way the staff interact with customers. It is also in sync with the image of the brand. Once a product is purchased the packaging corresponds with the brand, the web site corresponds, the way the help desk answers calls corresponds and so on.

Much care and thought are applied to ensure consistency between the different elements that are present in the customers' interaction journey. The embedding of a strong culture (encompassing an internal mechanism to communicate its values) ensures that all participants are aligned and that the cultural values are always the point of reference.

3. Structure

Building a structure which will automatically generate the right behaviours is often undervalued, yet it is critical. This can either apply to the structure of the company from an ownership perspective or the structure from an organisational chart perspective. Take the example of Vanguard. Vanguard is one of the most successful asset management firms globally.

Its founder Jack Bogle used to say that at Vanguard "Strategy follows structure"[3]. What he meant was that because the firm operates under a mutual structure, and is therefore owned by the investors themselves, the organisation as a whole works only toward the benefit of one group: its investors. This drives the entire culture of the organisation and the way it does business: from the way it builds products, to the way it services customers, to the way it talks and communicates with its clients. Controlling costs becomes a structural foundation, as opposed to a tactic. All is purpose built for the maximum benefit of customers.

The organisational design will also drive behaviours which can take many forms. It can be the way people share profits or rewards. Creating a firm with partners interested in the profits will have implications, for instance. It can be the way organisational charts are devised; how verticality is arranged to ensure greater control or greater empowerment. It can be the design of key performance measures aimed at rewarding specific behaviours or outcomes.

The point here is that the way an organisation operates and is structured will have a direct effect on the brand because the behaviours of the people within the organisation will be affected by this design, which will in turn have an impact on outcomes, affecting customers and their perception of the brand.

4. Image and communications management

This is the most obvious area, the one covered in text books and dinner conversations (and certainly a preferred topic

3 John C Bogle, Common sense on Mutual funds. Published by John Wiley & Sons.

among marketers). Most of these conversations are centred around the value of creativity and of its entertainment value 'great ad!', but do not be fooled. One should be aware that great brands have one secret weapon and only one: they express their difference. Both in terms of art and science the expression of this difference is crucial. Not only does it define a point of distinction within the category and against competitors, this difference must coincide with customers' expectations.

In other words, you can tick all the right boxes but if customers do not understand, or are not open to, your value proposition the brand will not be successful. The value proposition must be relevant and connected with customers' needs and aspirations. This is why I mention the art of expressing the difference, mostly by creating something new and distinguishable, and the science, by ensuring that value propositions resonate in customers' minds and wallets.

Forget about great ads from an entertainment value point. Think about communication from a strategic point of view. At a high level your brand communication must:

a. Reflect the brand value proposition (in all its aspects)
b. Be noticeable
c. Be relevant.

A 'great ad', or what I would prefer to refer to as an effective communication, is a communication that ticks all three boxes. Your ad should be a great ad only if that is what is required to convey the value proposition, ensure that you are seen by your target audience and is relevant and therefore actionable. I provide specific details in the chapter: *Best practice communication strategy*.

5. Business intelligence

The brand must be part of the business, not some strange concept with a life of its own. As with the rest of the business, the key brand drivers and their impact on customers and prospects must be managed and monitored. For example brand managers must understand their customer behaviours and attitudes, the market they are part of, and they must monitor the impact of their own activities. They must have both a short term view because customers can change rapidly and a long term view to provide perspective. There must be a system in place to gather and monitor business intelligence. Your brand must be guided by your vision first but the monitoring of your impact should provide clues that may steer your direction.

There may be a time when the brand leaders' intuitions or decisions are confronting and go against what the research or the data indicates. When this situation arises those developing the brand are in a position to make a deliberate choice in order to act in a certain way acknowledging the risks they are taking and the contradictions they are confronting. In this way they become cognisant of the variables surrounding their decisions, the impact of their decisions and the need to monitor.

Leadership and Culture Needs to be led from the top and reflected throughout the organisation. *e.g. Richard Branson*	**Structure** Organisational structure drives behaviour.*e.g. Credit Unions*
Business Intelligence	
Vision and Purpose What do you have to offer? *e.g. Industry Super Funds*	**Image and Communication Management** Express your difference. All touch points need to be considered. *e.g. ING Direct*

So what about the products? The products or services are a direct output of the vision and purpose. Whatever category or market in which the brand is active, the role of the brand is to add value and to differentiate the products. Alternately, the products must be built according to the brand values, which themselves derive from the vision and purpose. There is a double interaction. Products are built according to the purpose of the brand and the brand's role is to support the product diffusion irrespective of which came first, the product or the brand.

Best of breed example: **Virgin**

Virgin is a particularly interesting organisation to study. In many ways it can be equated with a branding venture capital organisation licensing the Virgin brand name. In some instances it is just a branding licence (e.g. Virgin Mobile in Australia) operated by another organisation. What is rare is that it covers a spectrum of industries including music, mobile phones, finance, insurance, credit cards, fitness and air transport. The Virgin brand has been able to carry its unique value proposition over a spectrum of industries and categories. It is also interesting in the way it has treated its branding from a look and feel point of view. The Virgin logo (the words within particular font treatment and colour) is consistent, however other aspects vary from category to category and geography to geography to suit the target audiences. The brand standards, from a look and feel point of view, are very flexible, even loose. From a design perspective, however, the brand is tight. The nature of the brand, its value proposition remains. Another joining block is the fact that it has a face (Richard Branson) and a specific tone of voice. Its brand values are clear, and the brand revolves around nurturing those values. It therefore matches our criterion of a) reflecting the

41

brand value proposition b) being noticeable and c) being relevant in the categories and markets with which it is involved.

Best of breed example: **Apple**

Apple represents a great case study for anyone looking at a successful branding story. In particular, the absolute devotion of some of its customers, who await and celebrate the release of new products, is a phenomenon in itself. Many studies and books have been written on this subject. However, if you juxtapose the fundamental components of brand development and management, you will find that the essential components we have been examining are omnipresent.

Apple was created at a time when the counter culture movement was blossoming. The essence of the counter culture movement was to be radically different to what was perceived as the blandness and reactionary vision of the prevailing American culture at the time. It was in direct opposition to mainstream conformity. When hair was short the counterculture movement proponents grew their hair. When people in the mainstream wore pleated trousers and white shirts they wore jeans and loud T-shirts. When computers were complex, bulky and fairly unattractive, they created Apple ... simple, stylish and user friendly. They created a brand whose philosophy was to be different. Making good use of a technological marvel that the mainstream had created, they applied the counter culture approach by building something that appeared radically different even if it was based on a similar technological foundation. That approach was applied to many aspects of their products, especially the design, the simplicity and the user friendliness.

Like other aspects of the counter culture the brand became "cool". Owners of Apple computers became, through their purchase, part of a different group of individuals. They belonged to the Mac tribe, the cool tribe. This is particularly important because sociologists define the emergence of "cool" in the 20th and 21st centuries as a new form of social status. Did Mac users suddenly change their social status because of an Apple purchase? Perhaps not. But they certainly bought some cool factor. From a brand perspective creating the Apple difference was the key to success, it led to living the difference. The brand's success wasn't born out of a marketing campaign or a tag line. It was a way of building and presenting computers. The Apple computers were built the Apple way and as part of the Apple philosophy; it became a fully-fledged strategy. The brand was also led from the top, Steve Jobs was the embodiment of the Apple difference, inside and outside the walls of the organisation. Add the other elements – the fact that today Apple is a giant multinational computer and electronic manufacturer that is still able to carry its cool and different image – and it is clear that from a brand management perspective this is a real achievement. The marketing communication strategy is leveraging the core elements of the brand promise across the entire customer experience. Having now become mainstream itself it is difficult to carry on the point of difference. This means that, for marketers and business leaders, the future of the brand will become as much a case study as Apple's past has been. So, to be continued ...

66

Whatever your message is, it needs to
be believable. It needs to make sense to
the audience so they can relate to it."

CHAPTER 6

Best practice communication strategy

Leading managers of brands use a rigorous strategic approach to communication, encompassing 5 key elements. My study of the successful brand communication strategies, coupled with years of practice, has allowed me to develop the Archetypal brand foundation concept™. This concept defines what are the fundamental, and, should I say, non-negotiable elements necessary to developing effective brand communication. The Archetypal brand foundation concept is not about defining single pieces of communication but rather about identifying the strategic foundation on which to build the communication process. It comprises five key elements: Relevance, Clarity, Differentiation, Believability and Continuity.

Archetypal brand foundation concept™

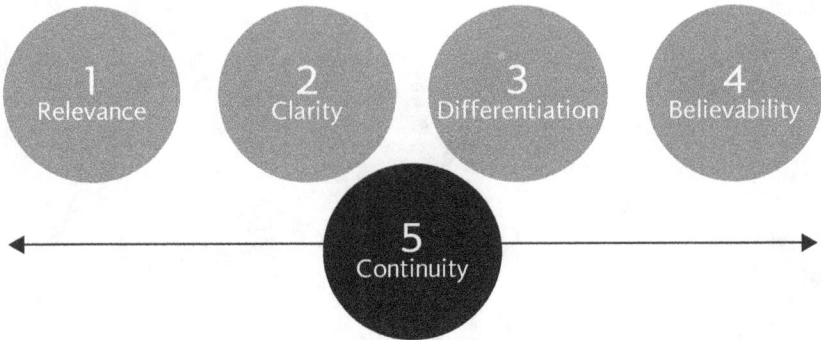

The science of communication

What does this mean in practice? When defining the communication strategy that will develop the brand message one needs to take into account the different elements in order to build the message, or the story, that is to be communicated.

Relevance: Consumers do not care about your brand, they care about themselves. The brand is one of the many means at their disposal to get what they need want or desire. The brand's story therefore needs to resonate with consumers and prospective consumers otherwise it will just be additional noise in a crowded communication space.

Clarity: This is about message clarity, being clear about what we want to say and how we want to say it. The brand owner must know intimately what they want to convey. The role of the brand owner is to know the 'what'. Other support entities such as designers, copywriters, ad agencies, PR agencies, e-communication agencies, social media agencies etc. will support the 'how'. Marketers and business leaders who leave the 'what' to their consultants or agencies are in fact relinquishing brand ownership. If they allow consultants and agencies to take over, the ownership will come to belong to someone else. Often the essence of the brand will get lost, creating a domino effect that can ultimately destroy the brand.

Differentiation: As I mentioned, this is the key. I would argue that this is the point, the objective of branding. Your brand must be different and so must be your communication, strategy and delivery. Communicate your difference.

Believability: Whatever your message is, it needs to be believable. It needs to make sense to the audience so they can relate to it. The big banks in Australia have historically failed spectacularly at it. While they all tell us how different they are and how amazingly customer-centric and trustworthy they are, research shows that customers have opposite views. The banks are more often than not disliked and seen as greedy. Smaller banks in particular have been able to leverage this by proposing simple, straight forward and down to earth value propositions – like Bendigo and Adelaide Bank, which is seen much more favourably by customers. The interesting fact here is that big Australian banks, despite their open pursuit of profit, have a lot to offer to the community. But they have a tendency to attempt to push messages that do not ring true and which at the end of the day do little to differentiate them. One particular area where they sometimes succeed is their messaging on pricing strategies. Certainly these are of a tactical nature but they drive real results because, interestingly, they are Relevant, Clear, and Believable, and sometimes Different.

The brand quiz: Can you tell which bank says what? Do you believe the message? Does it coincide with your perception of the brand?

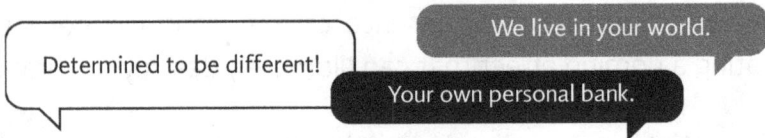

> Determined to be different!

> We live in your world.

> Your own personal bank.

Continuity: While less important for tactical activities, continuity is crucial to build and sustain a brand. There needs to be continuity in tone, style, value proposition and in overall delivery of the brand promise. The reality is that business leaders, and especially marketers, quickly get bored with their own messages or have a tendency to believe that their messages need to be constantly refreshed. Yet there is much research to demonstrate that message refreshing is not always necessary and can even be counter-productive. What is at stake here is the ability to convey a value proposition over the longer term, to embed it in the psyche of customers and prospects. Repetition and consistency are two means to achieve this. This does not mean that all communication remains the same, but the direction of the communication and its delivery form remain relatively constant. Think about great brands like Coca Cola for a moment. They use different ads to cater for different segments. However many elements of the communication remain constant and last over long periods of time, like the tag lines, the use of the logo, and the expression of the feeling of satisfaction that the product generates.

Brands must be looked at from a longitudinal perspective because the essence of the brand must be carried through over time to reinforce its legitimacy and to ensure that the brand values are embedded in the minds of consumers and stakeholders. A brand can be built rapidly, but its success over time depends on the ability to carry its core value proposition and its core promise – time and time again. Consistency is a necessary element to drive believability.

The art of communication

The delivery of the message, of the value proposition, is, in its own particular way, a form of art. It requires the mastering of communication techniques and a dose of creativity. Not a noble art perhaps. More a practical one focused on a defined outcome. If we know that great brands generate both a rational response and an emotional response, the communication must support the delivery of these two drivers. The balance between the two is generated by a number of factors or variables which brand owners and marketers need to understand in order to succeed. The type of product, the category, the customer segments, the reigning attitudes, the competitive environment, the competitive messaging are some of the key factors to consider to find the right balance. Depending on what side of the fence you sit, some will have a tendency to argue that real brand or product benefits should be the key drivers while others will believe in the unique power of emotions. If the answer was obvious we would not have so many debates. The reality

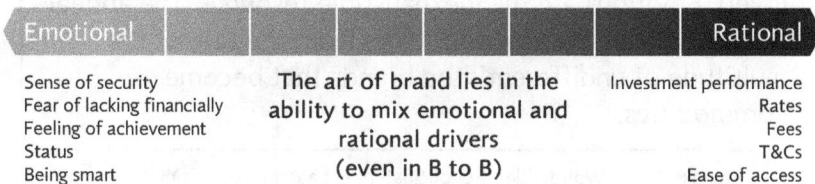

Emotional		Rational
Sense of security Fear of lacking financially Feeling of achievement Status Being smart	**The art of brand lies in the ability to mix emotional and rational drivers (even in B to B)**	Investment performance Rates Fees T&Cs Ease of access

49

is that each brand must be assessed individually. In all cases, however, both drivers must be weighted and considered. Each communication activity must be integrated with this thinking. This can result in different pieces of communication being weighted according to different drivers, which works well as long as there is a coherent thread between them.

The art of developing a brand, therefore, lies in the ability to mix emotional and rational drivers. Even in business to business communication emotions play an integral part. While we all think that we make rational decisions, our psychological makeup means that we are at all times influenced by our wishes and desires, that which we fear, the real things that drive us, who we love. Human psychology is complex but if we use the hypothesis that, at a very high level, both rational and emotional drivers play a role in all decisions, it helps us with our communication technique. This does not mean that all communication pieces must include both, but it does mean that there is a role for both in the overall approach to communication. For example, in asset management institutional sales, where billions of dollars are bought and sold, a dry looking proposal as opposed to a glossy proposal may in some cases support the feeling of seriousness.

> ...the consumer is loyal to "beyond reason". Like Apple, Coca-Cola, Nike...Respect is only a condition for admission into the competition. The challenge is to be loved. Emotions are the inexhaustible resource. The appeal to emotions, is the way to escape from the fate of the multitude of undifferentiated brands that become commodities.
>
> Kevin Roberts, Worldwide CEO of Saatchi & Saatchi Advertising

It may create depth and trust when set against competitors who may be seen as too sales-based and lacking in real depth, which can engender a feeling of distrust or suspicion.

There is no doubt that the power of emotions is incredibly strong and I would tend to agree with Kevin Roberts (on the previous page). But it is not always the whole story.

I cannot quote 'admen' without issuing some form of friendly warning. It is important to contextualise the emotional appeal and not confine it to the advertising bucket:

> *Warning:*
> Emotional does not mean funky advertising. It means that the brand promise goes beyond the immediate nescessity of the product. It meets an expectation of outcome, of achievement, how small or big it may be, resulting in a feeling of satisfaction.

The core message. It is necessary to mention that when communicating to your audience, even when launching or promoting the brand, it is not always necessary to speak about the brand. Marketing or sales campaigns can promote a particular product and only emphasize messages around that product yet still build the brand. The brand needs to be present for customers and prospects to differentiate and recognize your product, but it does not need to be the core message. The product may be the sales driver and the brand simply an identifier.

"

Brand building will follow from how
you communicate and how you
manage the purchase experience."

CHAPTER 7

Mediums of communication

Too often brand communication is linked to advertising. I would like to demystify this concept. When advertising is the chosen path, the most costly aspect of brand promotion lies in the cost of purchasing media. Good media buying is where I believe brand campaigns are often won or lost. It is often underestimated, unloved and outsourced. And media buying is full of myths and misconceptions.

Myths: Mediums of communication to build a brand

Myth number 1: The first myth to demystify is that to build a brand you need what marketers call "above the line" media. Above the line refers to readily available mediums such as television, radio, outdoor and aspects of the internet. The reality is that brand communication must be built on only one premise: it must be a medium that your target audience will look at or listen to. This could well be TV, but it could simply be your sales force talking to people, or it could be your direct marketing.

Myth number 2: You need a brand message or campaign to build your brand. In reality, a series of direct communication campaigns that sell a particular product or product line may be enough to build your brand. Certain mediums of communication will be strong at delivering an immediate call to action, driving prospects to buy your product. Brand building will follow from how you communicate and how you manage the purchase experience.

Myth number 3: Leave it to the media buyer: Most media buyers have an enormous amount of knowledge and know-how about how to purchase media. However, they often employ the same "recipes" across clients, which results in competitors buying similar media in similar formats from similar media providers. Marketers and brand owners must drive their difference through the media buying process. Often it is the most expensive part of a brand campaign that requires particular attention.

The mediums of communication through which you will communicate your brand value proposition have to be based on your potential customers and your customer segments. What this means is that different segments can be more reactive to certain mediums. In most cases their habits of media consumption will vary. Therefore a thorough understanding of your target market is critical for media selection. Customers and potential customers will have common media consumption patterns but there will also be points of difference. One very major point of difference is that with your customers, the direct channels of communication must play a leading role.

A number of considerations drive the media strategies of successful brands. There is not one panacea to media buying.

Mediums of communication

A number of key considerations require attention when devising the media approach. They can be summarised as:

- Media consumption: How are my segment(s) gathering information within and outside the category my brand is involved with?

- What is the most cost effective manner to reach my segments? This may be an ongoing question which will vary in time and according to the objective you have. Should you want to drive a particular area of brand awareness? This may drive a very different approach to driving an immediate call to action.

- What is the optimal cross medium approach?

- How many times do I need to communicate to drive awareness, familiarity, consideration or action?

- What mediums are most linked to my brand?

- What mediums are better suited to carry my message?

- Importantly, these questions are not to be asked once. They should be asked each time you create a communication objective.

"

Your brand must be guided by your vision first but the monitoring of your impact should provide clues that may steer your direction."

CHAPTER 8

Brand architecture

Sub-brands can be brands belonging to a wider brand, a category of products or a brand that shares the same core mission and purpose as the wider brand but which has its own flavour and slightly different personality. They are used to attract a different target audience, or to offer a different pricing or servicing structure.

Depending on the organisation's objective, sub brands can be directly or loosely associated with the wider brand. Examples of close association include brands like ING (master brand) and ING direct (sub brand). Examples of loose associations include brands like NAB (master brand) and UBank (sub brand). In many instances products can act as sub brands, meaning that they are recognizable entities by themselves, and are associated with a unique set of attributes. Sub brands are particularly useful when an organisation is involved with different product categories, sub categories or niche markets. Or it may wish to attract different population segments. For example, the

Centurion card, which is marketed separately, was created by American Express to attract higher net worth individuals. Product based sub brands such as a (Ford) Fiesta versus a (Ford) Focus (note that car makers would call both the Fiesta and the Focus brands) can share more or less the DNA of the Ford brand (reliability, for example) while having their own distinctive traits and appealing to different audiences or market segments. They will, however, always have an impact on the overall brand. These sub brands can never be considered in isolation. They must share, and be integrated with, the main brand attributes, the unique brand differentiator. For example, the (Apple) iPod and the (Apple) Macs are sub brands with particular traits that will appeal to different segments. But they share the Apple core brand attributes of design and simplicity.

When the products' sub-brands are starting to deviate from the core brand attributes, the multi brand approach, whereby specific stand-alone brands are created, becomes a useful strategy. This strategy enables the integrity of the core brand to be maintained while, at the same time, enabling a diversification of product lines. It provides the ability to reach very different target audiences. It is an approach that encompasses the notion of brand architecture whereby different brands form part of a simple or complex set within a master brand. The master brand may be a corporate entity like Procter & Gamble, which can support existing individual brands carrying their specific product range. Or the master brand can be an existing client-facing and product-owning brand such as Westpac, which works alongside its many Australian icon brands such as BT Financial Group, Bank of Melbourne, St George, RAMS, and BankSA. (One could argue that the master brand is Westpac Group but because the word Westpac is present in both instances we will consider it the master brand).

Brand architecture: Which is the most successful: single brand approach or multi brand approach? There is little use falling into this debate. If there was one approach superior to another we would know it by now. What is clear is that different approaches fit different purposes. So the question should rather be: 'When should one organisation choose one approach versus the other?'

Different options:

- The master brand (defined here as the brand under which all other brands fall in the brand architecture hierarchy) is only a corporate brand. In this instance, the value of the master brand lies in its creation of shareholder value. The brand adds little or no value to the sub brands in terms of customer appeal and value proposition. The luxury goods brand LVMH is an example of this strategy. LVMH owns brands like Louis Vuitton, which does not need the support of the master brand and may even be devalued if there is too much association with another brand, especially if it is of the size of LVMH.

- The master brand is a driver of sub brands. In this approach the brand association of the master brand with the sub brand provides real added value to the sub brand. Virgin represents a successful example. By using the name Virgin on a raft of very diverse businesses, the company provides instant recognition and brand association.

- The master brand acts as a support to the sub brand. This approach provides a form of support in terms of strength or credibility, while not intrinsically driving the primary value of the sub brand. In financial services the Westpac brand provides financial credibility to its sub brands, like Bank of Melbourne and St George.

- There are cases in between where the master brand provides some level of support that may affect specific segments or markets. It is interesting to note how some brands in the fast moving consumer goods sector are increasing their presence alongside their sub brands. One needs to consider that the reverse also occurs, in the sense that the sub brand may provide credibility to the master brand, especially when the sub brands are the only public-facing brands. In this case, the association with icon brands benefits perceptions about the master brand.

Brands apart: HSBC versus Westpac. There are continuous debates about the pros and the cons of one overarching brand strategy versus a multi brand approach (I do not wish to discuss the business strategy component here but rather focus on the branding component of this strategy, while acknowledging that they are associated). HSBC and Westpac are on the opposite sides of the spectrum. The first, HSBC, has one global brand that transcends geographies and remains consistent across regions, markets and languages. The second, Westpac, has developed a number of brands in the Australian financial services industry that both compete with and complement each other. What the two organisations have in common is that both strategies have proven to be successful to date. HSBC is carrying its brand message consistently, appealing to similar markets across different geographies. Westpac is catering for a number of different segments within the Australian financial services industry. From a branding execution perspective HSBC's one brand strategy is executed to cater for cultural and market differences with one single overarching approach. Needless to say, this is a complex exercise. What this provides, however, is the opportunity to build a brand footprint across a core target market in the different countries in which HSBC does business. This doesn't allow HSBC to cater for the subtleties of each market though. Nor can it be adapted for the various segments that compose each market. It is expendable, allowing the bank to expand to other markets with one single pre-established and repetitive model but it has limitations within each country. Of course, the segment's footprint could always be expanded in each country by assimilating other brands or by widening the product offering, even changing the business model while keeping the brand consistency.

For Westpac the challenge is the opposite. The organisation would need a very different approach to expand its brand outside its borders. It would need to use either one Westpac master brand, or expand the individual brands in markets in which the target segments are viable. In Australia, while the costs of running different brands might be greater than running one solo brand, the multi brand approach does offer the possibility to increase the footprint across a diverse range of customer segments and product categories, which one brand cannot offer. In a category dominated by four big players it provides an alternative approach. What it also provides for the financial group is brand diversification allowing the bank to reduce its dependency on one brand only. While financial institutions have a tendency to prefer the one solo brand, in the post GFC days of heightened risks, when there is an increased requirement to gain access to market segments, this does provide a useful diversification.

When looking at the brand strategies of these two impressive organisations, the conclusion that we can reach is that each strategy services a specific business model. The models are different, so are the brand strategies. Each approach enables the development of growth business strategies for each group, taking into consideration the particularities and markets available to both. This shows how each brand **strategy must be completely linked to the business model**. One supports the other.

"

Consumers do not care about your brand,
they care about themselves. The brand is
one of the many means at their disposal
to get what they need, want or desire."

CHAPTER 9

Areas of consideration

The critical moments or moments of truth. We need to place special emphasis on the customer experience as an intrinsic part of brand management. When looking at the customer's or prospect's experience, we must consider independently the combination of direct and indirect interactions that affect the customer experience. In an ideal scenario all interactions are consistent with the brand promise: from the advertising message, the contact with the sales person, to the welcome pack, the call centre staff, the billing mechanism, the customer feedback process and the after sales service. There are, however, contact points at particular times, called critical moments, which are more significant than others. They will have a greater impact on the customer's perception of the brand. We can consider these as 'moments of truth' because the brand proposition is being truly tested. As with all tests they will generate a conscious or unconscious rating in the minds of customers.

These critical moments must first be identified and then be managed, ideally in a predefined fashion. An adequate or inadequate response (in the eyes of the customer) will positively or negatively impact the overall customer perception towards the brand, not just the customer's perception of the specific event. We need to note that these critical moments include personal interactions, all forms of communications (marketing, operational, PR, social, web, servicing, billing) and how customers perceive the physical product dimensions such as features and packaging. When customers purchase a product they "interact" with the product, meaning that it is not possible to dissociate this experience from the overall brand experience; it is integral to it. For example, if your product has a weakness such as being difficult to initially set up, this has the potential to have a negative impact on the brand perception (obvious but so often true). Managing this weakness appropriately with, for example, a printed instruction manual that is very pleasing to the eye and extremely easy to read and understand, or making an additional version available on the website for those who cannot find their printed version, or providing a free phone number with a friendly operator to call if needed, may negate this entirely. It can even potentially enhance the brand perception despite the initial difficulties.

In a similar way to personal interactions, the initial product interaction requires a positive outcome. This experience is always a critical moment. From a brand management perspective (not just a product feature perspective) the set up mechanism in our example should become as seamless as possible and be incorporated in the product evolution itself. Think of Apple. You can see how the set up mechanism for their products can become a tangible product feature, a key differentiator and a brand reinforcement.

Areas of consideration

How do you define the moments of truth? The most rigorous method is to follow the entire road to purchase and post-purchase experience, mapping it step by step. It is necessary to define all the points of interaction and analyse their various levels of importance. Start from the point of view that all interactions or points of contact are important, so none should be left unchecked. Then define the ones that are likely to affect the customers more than the others. Once this is done rank all interactions as 1. Critical 2. Very important and 3. Relatively important. This will provide a list of prioritisation to identify where to place the most emphasis and effort. Also, consider the fact that the sum of interactions, in other words the overall experience, must be viewed as a critical moment of truth. So let's use a simplified example. In this example we ask a few questions in order to help us understand the variables attached to each interaction enabling us to rate them:

- The prospect starts looking at the initial advertising (What particular message, look and feel, where does he or she see the advert?)

- He/she then attempts to find the product via a reseller (What method does he/she use, how easy is it?)

- Entering a store he/she experiences the surroundings (What experience does this generate?)

- He/she then waits for a sales person (How long is he/she waiting?)

- He/she is greeted by a sales person (How? How amicable is the sales person and what is the general appearance and demeanour of the sales person?)

- They start interacting (What is the sales person's sales process?)

- The prospect is eyeing and touching the product for the first time (How is the product presented?)

- The prospect makes the purchasing decision (How long after entering the store? Is there any particular moment that can be seen?)

- Paying (Are modes of payment offered, are there additional charges? Are credit facilities available?)

- The prospect is now a customer and sets up the product (How easy is it? How long does it take?)

- First usage of the product (How easy is the packaging to use? How pleasing? What special features are there?)

- Calling the sales support (How easy is it to find the number? How long does it take to speak to an operator? How friendly and knowledgeable is the operator?)

- Receiving a welcome letter (How well written and relevant is it? Does it add value?)

- Receiving the first bill (Are there any surprises? Problems with accuracy? Is information easy to find?)

- Is the look and feel in synch with the rest of the communication and product?

- Experiencing the product more in depth (How does the product impact or fit into everyday life?)

All these are points of contact with the brand and require an in-depth analysis and scenario testing. All these individual interactions will create a lasting impression of the brand. The overall experience, the sum of these interactions, will define how the customer ranks the brand. Remember that an unchecked weakness can have a disastrous effect while a weakness properly managed can enhance your value proposition. When in doubt, an easy way to check your path and priorities is to experience the product purchase and ownership yourself.

The impact of customer service

Often (but not always) companies that have built great brands make clear mention of their customer service as a point of differentiation. It is curious that many companies place emphasis on it because today this is hardly a real differentiator. It is more a base line to do business. But what does customer service truly mean when it comes to brand and vision? It can be defined in many different ways depending on the channel of distribution. It can be demonstrated via different elements of the customer experience such as a great sales processes, effortless online processing, unmatched after sales service and policy, well-staffed customer phone service. What is common though, is that in order to understand what great customer service means, companies with great brands analyse and manage thoroughly the entire customer experience. They place particular emphasis on what the customer goes through on the road to purchasing. They invest in business intelligence, which not only encompasses business metrics but also includes customer experience metrics. The reason they do this is that if they want customers to connect emotionally with the brand they must also understand how they connect physically with the brand. That way, the emotion can be carried from the initial promise through to the sales experience, the service experience, the repeat purchase and to the customer potentially recommending the brand to someone else.

Perhaps the most notable customer experience that great brands have in common is based on the understanding and precise management of what needs to be delivered. One particular example of customer management experience comes to mind in the telecommunications category. The sales process is often of first quality. Products are explained, paper work rapidly processed (for some) and connection established rapidly (for some). The price is low, so the customer thinks he or she has made a good deal, and leaves the store happy. What comes after is a different story. It takes hours to connect to a customer service representative when an issue arises and there are issues with billing and reception.

Does this ring a bell? The calculation that organisations like these make is that they will differentiate only what is absolutely necessary to drive sales and maintain and grow the brand. The focus is only on what is a nice product to have. In fierce competitive markets, where price wars are constant, the expectation is that 'a good deal' may be sufficient to satisfy a segment of customers. If this segment is the brand's target market then the strategy will most likely be based on the understanding that the customer experience must be principally generated by feel good messaging and good sales process. In this instance, the costs of after sales customer service can be minimised without entirely destroying the brand perception.

Psychology at work–the principle of integration

When it comes to brand communication some design schools have been influenced by research and analysis from the Gestalt psychology school. In essence – and just limiting this notion to our core subject of brand communication – the Gestalt principle of perception is that images are interpreted as a sum of their parts as opposed to dissected into different elements. This led to many design practices that are now widely adopted, such as the use of balance in graphics, sizing, the arrangements of shapes and the synergy of colours. What this really means, though, is that the human psyche has a tendency to group elements into one entity. For example, we tend to associate a trunk, dozens of branches and hundreds of leaves with one entity: a tree. This goes far beyond visual perception. The human mind groups together experiences that have common traits. We build connections between them to make them feel like one experience and we do it over and over. This process relates directly to all the various elements that constitute a brand. As discussed, a brand by itself does not really exist as one closed off entity. It is really the sum of its parts (product components and look and feel, communication, point of sales). Apply the principle of perception to brands and we can determine that all elements and interactions that impact a customer are grouped into one bucket: the brand experience. We do not need to understand this principle to know that a good experience reinforces the overall brand perception, and that a bad experience generates a negative impact. A mix of the two will lead to one view of the brand: positive, negative or mixed, depending on the impact that each experience had on the customer. This further reinforces the need for a consistent brand experience, especially the need for marketing integration when applied to brand communication.

Marketing integration is not, as some view it, making everything look similar. Rather, it is a mechanism to make every part of the communication and customer touch points congruent, synergistic, in a way that leads to the same brand values and positioning, whereby all the touch points with customers or prospects reinforce each other. In my experience this is where smart communicators have been able to get a real edge. Do not focus on all elements being the same, but instead focus on all elements pointing towards the same values, the same image of the brand, the same positioning. So, for example, if you pride yourself on customer service, ensure all your call centre staff are trained to provide the best service possible rather than insisting all call centre operators answer in the same way with exactly the same script, word for word. The operators must focus on the experience rather than on a repetitive and unfelt script.

In practice you should, more often than not, attempt to build the different outputs as closely as possible to one another. This creates synergy, reinforces the perceptual (e.g. visual) message and ensures a level of consistency. However, best practice communication must be viewed in terms of target markets and context. People in different target markets will respond differently to imagery, vocabulary and certain types of message expressions. Therefore the more adapted to your target market your communication is, the more relevant it becomes and the more likely it is to be successful. As well, your communication is constantly facing a dynamic environment. Your messages will differ according to the reality of this environment: competitor activity, sales trends, adoption levels of your brand, geographic, economic and political variables. The work that needs to be done, therefore, is to ensure that

Areas of consideration

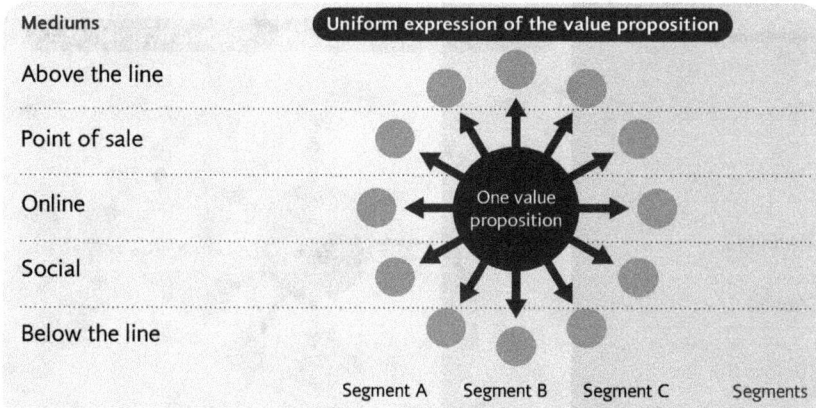

Mediums	Uniform expression of the value proposition			
Above the line				
Point of sale		One value proposition		
Online				
Social				
Below the line				
	Segment A	Segment B	Segment C	Segments

while the communication is adapted to the diverse market environments and target audiences; all communication is linked by a common thread that leads the customer to the same brand values. For example, if your point of difference is customer service, you might express it as 'red carpet' to an aspirational audience with glittery imagery; 'free call' to a value searching audience, with friendly imagery; or '24 hour support' with professional imagery to a B to B customer. But it should all lead to one conclusion: Great service.

In a perfect world, a perfect brand communication plan would look like the diagram above. One message is delivered across all customer touch points in a similar way.

The reality is that it is more like the graph on the next page. Segments have different levels of importance, messaging codes and servicing requirements. Product offerings may vary by segments or markets. Therefore the communication will evolve by segment, with the resulting effect that some channels and mediums of communication will have more impact than others. This will require different levels of message articulation.

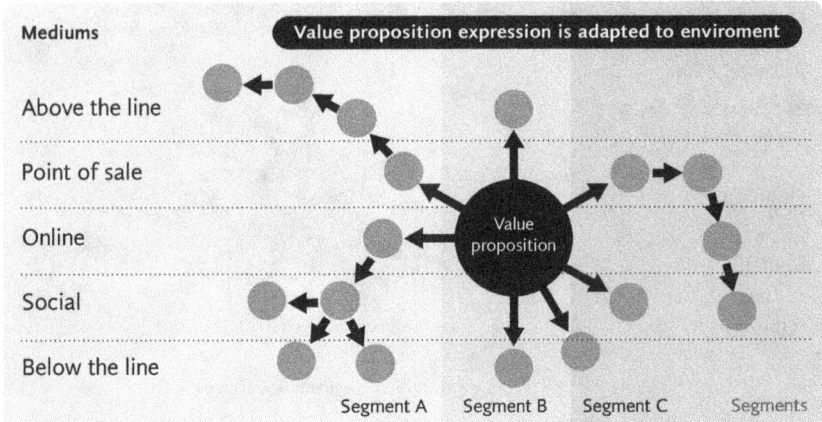

Mediums				
Value proposition expression is adapted to enviroment				
Above the line				
Point of sale				
Online			Value proposition	
Social				
Below the line				
	Segment A	Segment B	Segment C	Segments

What about social media?

The role of social media within brand communication must be considered to be like any other channel of communication. The reason for this is that each channel of communication performs a specific function and social media has its own. Do not get caught up in the fact that it is the fashionable channel, the 'channel du jour'. Brands did not wait for social media to exist to succeed, so do not expect social media to become the new panacea. The truth is that more organisations have failed than succeeded when attempting to build a solid return on investment from social media.

This is often true of a new channel of communication. Think how many websites failed to deliver in the early days until organisations really started to comprehend the true leverage they could provide? Take a deep dive into social media and you will find that it can deliver a real, incremental role in brand communication by providing an instant mechanism for the company to share information about the brand. More importantly, its unique function is to provide customers and influencers with the means to share their views on a scale vastly superior to traditional word of mouth. This has never been seen before.

It is social media's technological particularities and its multiple modes of engagement that provide true opportunities and threats for brands. Currently, this new form of media is gaining extremely rapid momentum, going through an early evolutionary phase. But the social media landscape of today is likely to differ tomorrow. What will remain constant in the near future, is that this channel will impact the communication spectrum through its capacity to reach large audiences in a relatively short time. The messages can evolve in all kinds of directions as with any real conversation. Social media creates a platform where, in essence, the organisation loses control of the message by enabling and empowering its customers and potential customers to provide their opinions openly and share them with a wider audience. Because the organisation loses control of the message, the message generation must be thought about differently. It is not the same as in a controlled environment. The message must be suitable for different audiences and situations in order to avoid misinterpretation should it be carried (for example re-twittered) further than its original destination. This is why some 'experts' talk about the customer 'owning the brand'; once they control the message they control the brand. In my view this is an exaggeration but what is not an exaggeration is that the message can impact the brand positively and negatively, sometimes in very fast and powerful ways.

One should decide if and how to enter social media by following the same principles of target audience media consumption. If

75

your target audience or a segment of your target audience is suitable, your approach will differ from a pure push communication strategy. In a sense this social media strategy will be closer to a PR or sales approach than a traditional brand communication approach. The reason for this is that in the social media world TRUE multi way communication can occur. In these instances the brand will be commented upon by external people, praised or criticised. Well managed, this can be a great medium for the promotion of the brand. It can be used as a continuous improvement process: for feedback management, reaction to issues, audience engagement, promoter encouragement. If it is not well managed however, it can have a negative effect on the brand. It can result in hollow responses, lack of engagement, repetitive messaging, slow response times, lack of integration with other mediums or brand messages, lack of continuity in the social media approach or loose processes. These can all affect the brand negatively.

The channel must always be considered when developing the communication strategy. Even if social media is not to be used by the organisation it may be used by external people interested in the brand or interested in an issue or element affecting the brand. If a social media channel becomes part of a pro-active communication strategy it must be integrated into your communication strategy and not thought about in isolation. This principle is valid for any channel of communication, social or not. Whilst some arguments may point to the fact that social media is an inherently different form of communication channel, I would argue that the same applies to most communication channels. *Each channel's particularity is the reason why you will choose to use it or not.* Using television is dramatically different to using direct mail, which in turn is different to using web, email, point of sale or events. It is the fact that they are different, that they approach and interact with customers in distinctive ways, that attracts organisations to use them in one fashion or another, to suit particular purposes and objectives. Social media is not 'more' different to the other communication channels, it is different full stop. It can be complementary when used in an integrated manner.

It also important to understand that social media is not one mechanism but an array of mechanisms. It consists of a collection of approaches using different tools with their own specificities, variations and mechanisms. The way you use and interact with twitter for example can be vastly different to your approach with LinkedIn which in turn will be different to YouTube, to Facebook, to Pinterest or to Blogger. In the same way the manner in which you interact with your own direct mechanism will be different to the way you approach external mechanisms.

As a new channel it does play a disruptive function (in its current electronic format). And it is continuously evolving. Interactions between customers, posting of comments, two way communications – none of this is new. What is new is the ease with which customers can share their thoughts, the speed at which they can communicate and the extended reach that they now can have. So what can this channel bring? There are many approaches and methods of engagement but at a high level it plays a number of roles. It is:

1. A source of information and monitoring
2. A campaign channel
3. A targeting mechanism

4. A relationship building instrument

5. A lead generation mechanism

6. An issue management tool

From a risk perspective you must consider

1. Potential negative feedback

2. Potential loss of control of the message

3. Speed of information

4. The need for real time monitoring

Social media can bring many benefits, and in an age when it is a 'trendy medium', brand managers must be wary of using it without a proper objective. The essential difference with this medium is that not only can it be a push communication channel, like traditional ones, it can be used as a pull channel as well. Customers, prospects or anyone can provide content.

Is this channel appropriate for my target audience?

This is the key question. Is my audience using this medium presently or could they and the brand benefit from using it? If the answer is yes, the next question is: How will your brand provide value through this channel, and what particular mode of engagement and distribution mechanism (e.g. Twitter, Facebook, LinkedIn etc.) will you use?

With social media your engagement cannot be half hearted. Dedication to the channel will be required due to the fact that it is a real time environment and there is a need for fresh content. Content needs to be produced regularly and interactions need to be monitored in real time so that any issue can be dealt with immediately. If this requires more resources than is possible, then a one-way channel may be another possibility. But here again, content must be produced regularly or the channel will become obsolete.

Like all mediums, social media can play an important role, and it must be thought about carefully, principally because it has speed, ease and a two way communication format. But remember the golden rule. You must be different to prevail. Doing the same thing as everyone else will not help you differentiate your brand, it will make you look the same. While you may use similar mechanisms and platforms, the core of your communication must always reflect who you are and what you stand for, no matter what method of engagement you choose.

"

Brand owners must place a special emphasis on the ability of the brand to keep its customers beyond the short term sales."

CHAPTER 10

Measurement

There are a number of ways to measure brand success. I will keep it extremely simple in order to define principles that can be implemented, as opposed to a detailed implementation process.

We can define four types of measurement for the brand that should be used:

1. Acquaintance

2. Strength

3. Perception

4. Corporate value

Acquaintance and Strength attributes tend to work in a logical progression. They define the brand's strength as the customer goes on the road to purchasing. These attributes are useful indicators to understand where the brand is pulling, or not pulling, its weight. The customer journey along the road to purchasing follows a specific path. A prospect needs to see your brand (awareness), what it has to sell or value it can offer (familiarity) before contemplating a purchase (consideration), deciding on the purchase (intent) and buying (purchase). Once the person has become a customer, he or she may re-purchase or buy another product of the brand (loyalty) and tell their best friends about the great buy (advocacy).

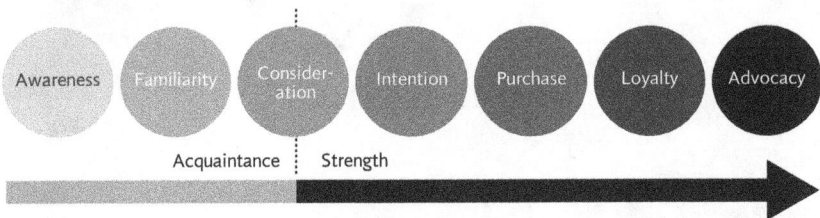

Note: It is possible to get more granular views by differentiating favourability from strength to stature etc. What needs to be understood is where customers and prospects are in the purchase cycle and how predisposed or favourable to the brand they are.

Acquaintance

Acquaintance relates to the concept of awareness (do you know this brand?) and familiarity (are you familiar with this brand?)

Awareness is the first step in the brand journey. For your brand to be adopted it must be seen (awareness) and then it must be known (familiarity). Therefore the tracking of these two measures provides an insight into which market is available at any point of time. The tracking indicates the availability of the market because there is a correlation between awareness, familiarity and purchase. The more prospects are familiar with your brand, the more likely it is that they will consider the brand or products, the more they will intend to purchase and the more likely it is that they will proceed with a purchase.

Familiarity is about perception, knowing the brand well enough to attach a value to it. It can be about perceiving the brand's values, what makes it different. Or it can be about what products or services it offers. Traditionally, brands will create a build-up of the awareness but there will be a lag in the build-up of the familiarity. Familiarity tends to grow more slowly because it requires the prospect to show interest in the brand or its offering 'I heard about the brand let me see what it's about'. Awareness can be a completely passive mechanism. The promotion of the brand can have immediate effects on awareness even if the prospect is not fully engaged in the promotional effort (such as passive listening). To achieve familiarity however, active listening or some form of engagement or interest in the brand is required.

Interestingly, long periods of time are not always necessary to build the acquaintance. If, for example, someone faces a retail shop they have never seen before with a brand they do not know, it will not stop them from entering the shop, discovering the brand, getting to know the product and adopting the brand immediately. Many online experiences are of a similar nature. The role of brands, however, is to move beyond the immediate appeal. It is to enable the building of a long term relationship and repeat purchases, to ensure that the products and services on offer can carry a premium, and ultimately to transform customers into advocates of the brand.

Strength

Strength is defined as the following: *consideration* (are you considering purchasing from this brand), *intention to purchase* (do you plan to purchase from this brand in the near future), *purchase* (real sales or sales mentions), *loyalty* (stickiness, cross and upsell) and finally **advocacy** (willingness to promote to others). In other words once prospects are familiar with the brand they will engage in the decision making process (consideration). The relative strengths of your brand will drive the level of intention to purchase for all those familiar with the brand. This intent will have different levels of strength. Assessing its intensity will help the brand owner understand the real power of the brand to "win the contest" against other brands or offerings. Monitoring the intention to purchase can also, in certain cases, be used to predict short-term future sales.

The next step is to measure the **purchase** levels and compare it with the previous attributes to understand the gap between the Acquaintance and Strength attributes. These must be viewed independently but tracking the relationship between them can also provide most interesting clues for brand owners. Understanding the size and nature of the gaps between each attribute will provide useful indications about why a brand or products are selling or not. It may drive the need for further data mining to understand the nature of gaps to define, for example, what stops a prospect, who intends to purchase, from actually activating the purchase.

Brand and sales are intrinsically related. *If your brand is not able to support the sales effort, then the brand is not performing its role.* Brand owners must look at specific components of the purchase (sales) data. It is an intrinsic part of the evaluation of the brand's success. This is critical. While the value of the brand is not solely about immediate sales it is also about immediate sales. The sales figures that brand owners must integrate are: overall sales and their breakdown by sub brands and products, the sales trends and, crucially for the brand activity, the market share. The market share relates to share against competitors overall, share against competitor for each market segment and share for each customer target group. It should be viewed in the present and as a trend. It also comprises share of wallet in these segments. This defines how well the brand is faring within its environment. It answers questions such as: 'Is your value proposition generating sales?' 'Are the sales above or below past sales?' 'Are they above or below specific competitors and the overall market?' 'Are these sales new customers to the category or are they against specific competitors?'

Out of this data will emerge two core insights:

- Brand effectiveness: What level of sales is the brand supporting? (Even if these are not always directly attributable to the brand they will be at least indirectly attributable)

- The contextual view: How is your brand rating against other brands?

Loyalty

Most marketers and senior managers know that acquiring a customer costs more than keeping a customer who repurchases. Therefore brand owners must place a special emphasis on the ability of the brand to keep its customers beyond the short term sales. The value proposition of the brand must support the short term sales but it must also build the brand acceptance beyond this first step. This is why the role of the brand owners is to create both a short and long term proposition. How do you judge if the longer term proposition is working? Loyalty analysis is a step in this direction. To support the brand strategy the brand owners will need to look at the following categories:

1. Longevity of customers; considerable effort is spent acquiring customers but do they stay with you?

    a. How long do customers remain as customers?
    b. How does this compare to the market?

2. What is the amount and nature of repeat purchases?

    a. How frequent are repeat purchases?
    b. How recent are repeat purchases?
    c. What is the monetary value of repeat purchases?

3. Upsell ratios & Cross sell ratios.

    a. How many customers purchase other products?
    b. How many customers increase their portfolio of products?
    c. How many customers increase the monetary value of their purchases?

4. Lifecycle value. By understanding how long customers are retained and the amount and frequency of repeat purchases, the cross sell and upsell ratios can be derived by a view of the value of customers over time. This can be broken down by segments or assessed overall.

5. Attrition ratios

    a. How many customers stop repurchasing (the brand or specific products)?
    b. How many customers defect to another brand?
    c. How many close their accounts or sever the relationship?

6. Churn ratios are critical to manage profitability and assess the strength of the value proposition once a customer adopts

the brand. Basically, the churn ratio shows whether you are running an "empty bucket".

   a. How many new customers come in compared to how many go out?

These are used in the analysis of general marketing or sales ratios, but they must be incorporated in the brand analysis. They provide valuable information on the behaviour of customers and therefore the extent to which the brand can drive certain behaviours. If, for example, the churn rate is high, the brand owner must understand the reasons. Where is the dissonance between the value proposition of the brand that attracted customers and the reality of the customer experience? Why are they coming and why are they leaving?

Perception

This relates to the attributes that customers or prospects associate with your brand. They can consist of specific attributes relating only to your brand. Or they can consist of a number of attributes and variables that affect your market environment or category and how your brand and competitors rate against each attribute.

This can be done using different methods: practical ones that include the scoring of perceptual variables (for the brand only, or against competitors) or, for more visual individuals, perceptual mapping, where the brand and its competitors are rated against different attributes. This enables the brand manager to understand the strength and weakness of the brand, how it is perceived by customers or prospects and how it compares with competitors.

Perception attributes help the brand owners to define how customers and prospects perceive the brand both in isolation and in the context of the environment. It is particularly useful for defining whether the perception of the brand matches the values of the brand. Perception attributes are many but often encompass attributes such as trust, leadership, value for money, cost leadership, service and thought leadership.

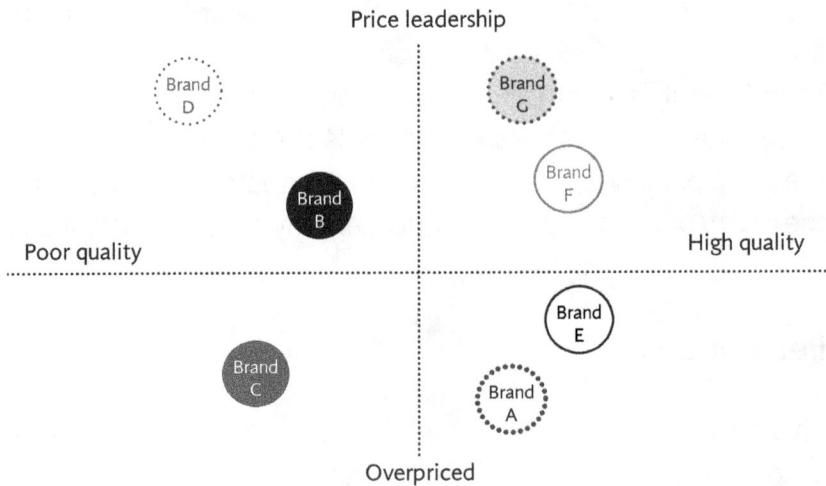

Corporate value

This relates to the value add that the brand brings to the organisation. Principally you want to consider the way in which your brand drives sales and adds a premium (a price premium, for example). The simple question is 'What would happen if you removed or changed the brand name from your products?' 'What impact would it have on sales , operations and pricing?'

The other key question is 'What is the value of the brand to the organisation as an intangible asset?' In this instance, the analysis is about defining:

Measurement

- What is the current portion of intangible revenues attributable to the brand and what is its potential value going forward (future revenues or earnings)?

- What is the cost of building the brand asset or of rebuilding the brand asset from the start?

- What is the market valuation as determined by how similar brands are valued by the financial markets?

The value of the brand as an asset to the company can be derived from the responses to these questions. This analysis will provide an understanding of the value created by a brand in generating consumer demand and driving future revenue streams. It can also increase an organisation's market value through the intangible asset value attributable to the brand value.

66

The brand is a psychological concept
and one must always keep in mind
that the physical attributes of the
products that the brand supports will be
judged by consumers in relation to the
perception that the brand creates."

CHAPTER 11

Final word

Brands are created to support and enhance the value proposition of organisations and their products and services. The foundation for building and sustaining successful brands is based on simple principles, although implementation can evolve into a more complex process that involves a number of areas of focus. This should not deter managers. The complexity should be relative to the needs and resources of the business. The main thing to remember is that the foundation of brands is the extent to which they create the ability to be different. Expressing your brand's difference and delivering on this difference will allow your brand to stand out. Start by being different and evolve the brand as your needs dictate. Follow the five brand building principles to provide a solid framework for you and your team: Vision and culture / Leadership and purpose / Structure / Image and communication management / Business intelligence.

No matter what consultants will tell you, there are no other 'silver bullets'. Your difference is both your risk and your opportunity. The brand is a psychological concept and one must always keep in mind that the physical attributes of the products that the brand supports will be judged by consumers in relation to the perception that the brand creates. We know that the best products will not always win and that, business considerations apart, strong brands provide a material advantage for organisations, helping them to develop and sell the value proposition of their products or their services. Brands cannot be ignored. If nurtured with care they can represent a formidable asset.

Enjoy your brand, enjoy the journey.

Index

C

Index

Index

M

N

O

P

Index

S

T

Index

U

UBank 57
uniqueness 3
upsell ratios 86

V

value 2, 3, 18, 19, 20, 25, 30, 31, 32, 39, 41, 42, 47, 48, 49, 54, 59, 68, 69, 73, 78, 81, 82, 83, 84, 85, 86, 87, 88, 89, 91, 92
value proposition 20, 30, 39, 41, 42, 48, 49, 54, 59, 69, 85, 86, 87, 91, 92
values 10, 36, 37, 41, 49, 72, 73, 83, 88
Vanguard 37, 38
variables 16, 23, 24, 26, 27, 28, 40, 49, 67, 72, 87
Virgin 41, 59
Virgin Mobile 41
vision 6, 15, 16, 19, 30, 34, 35–104, 36, 36–104, 36–104, 40, 41, 42, 56, 69, 91
Vision 35–104
Vision and purpose 35–104
vision statements 36–104
visualising 26

W

wants 2, 31
web site 32, 37
Westpac 58, 59, 60, 61
World Intellectual Property Organisation 3

Y

YouTube 77

www.ingramcontent.com/pod-product-compliance
Lightning Source LLC
Chambersburg PA
CBHW070155310326
41914CB00100B/1937/J

"A necessary and empowering resource for anyone considering counseling and hoping to enter a meaningful and healing therapy journey. Dr. Terri Watson intentionally guides the reader through each step of the therapy process, while giving careful consideration to both the dynamics of the therapeutic relationship and a holistic understanding of suffering and the change process."

Amanda M. Blackburn, vice president of student affairs and professor of counseling at Richmont Graduate University in Chattanooga, Tennessee

"Where do I even begin to try to find help? Do I need a Christian therapist? How do I know if I'm making progress? Dr. Watson tackles questions such as these with compassion, clarity, and a deep understanding of what potential or current clients need to know in order to find the best possible counselor for themselves as well as how to make the most of their therapeutic journey. A must-read!"

Heather Davediuk Gingrich, director of the MA counseling ministries degree at Toccoa Falls College, author of *Restoring the Shattered Self,* and coauthor of *Skills for Effective Counseling: A Christian Integration*

"Musicians understand their work is bigger than playing chords on a guitar, so they rely on intuitive, soulful presence to bring life to their art. Similarly, Dr. Terri Watson's latest book is technically excellent—drawing on current research and articulating the psychotherapy process with precision—but even more, she demonstrates the artistic wisdom of a seasoned clinician and educator. Yes, this is a vital book for those considering counseling or psycho-therapy, but it is also important that we therapists read it to remember who we are and why we do this work."

Mark R. McMinn, psychologist and coauthor of *An Invitation to Slow*

"Dr. Watson has provided a wonderful guide for the discernment of whether one needs professional counseling, how to choose a competent professional, and how to make the most of one's counseling journey. Even after being in the field for fifteen years, I benefited much from her wisdom and guidance and will recommend this broadly to friends and family members."

Eric M. Brown, assistant professor in the department of psychiatry at Boston University Chobanian and Avedisian School of Medicine

"For many, the decision to include a psychotherapist to journey through life's mystery, tragedy, and pain carries many questions and prompts hesitation. In *The Client's Guide to Therapy*, Dr. Terri Watson provides clarification, instills courage, and creates hope. Many who have observed the field of psychology and counseling for decades know Dr. Watson as the 'therapist among us.' It is fitting that she offers wisdom to any who are contemplating the journey within."

James Sells, Rosemarie S. Hughes Endowed Chair of Mental Health and Christian Thought at Regent University, and coauthor with Amy Trout and Heather Sells of *Beyond the Clinical Hour*